THE EXT LIFE OF GEORGE WASHINGTON:

A FOUNDING FATHERS BIOGRAPHY

BY: STEVEN WALLACE

Table Of Contents

George's Early Education 1

Washington's Pre-Revolutionary Military Career 8

Washington's Political And Religious Beliefs 11

The American Revolution 15

Revolution Strikes: The Battle For Democracy 21

After The War 25

Impact 31

The Mansions Of Rest 1797-1799 34

Conclusion 41

George's Early Education

George received his basic education at Rev. Mayre's Anglican school in Fredericksburg under a variety of tutors. He felt frustrated at home as an adolescent and felt oppressed by the confinement of domestic life. His stepbrother, Augustine Jr., knew that and had him move in with him and his wife, Anne Aylett, at Pope's Creek and attend school under a Mr. Williams. There Washington learned geography, history, and mathematics. Williams was fond of George and introduced him to James Genn, a land surveyor. Genn noted Washington's intellectual curiosity and took George with him when he went out on assignments. George liked the work. After he completed his studies at Mr. Williams' school, George returned home and occasionally visited with his other stepbrother, Lawrence. George always went to Lawrence for advice and support. At that time, George was restless and again felt an intense desire for independence and the need to break out on his own. When he told Lawrence about their mother's reaction when he tried to join the British Navy, Lawrence responded by saying that there would be many more opportunities besides the British Navy. After George mentioned that he had explored land surveying under a mentor, Lawrence suggested that he make the acquaintance of his wife's cousin, the elderly Lord William Fairfax of England, who was a land investor in the colonies. Fairfax was due to arrive shortly for a visit.

Fairfax liked George because he was a soft-spoken and polite boy, and they went hunting together. Lord Fairfax told Washington that he had recently purchased a number of land tracts in the Blue Ridge Mountains and wanted the land surveyed. That rekindled George's interest in surveying, and he talked excitedly with Fairfax about his experiences doing surveys while at Mr. Williams' school. George really loved the wild, unharnessed land. When he discussed this with his stepbrother, Lawrence suggested that he pursue surveying professionally.

Through Fairfax's connections, George attended the College of William and Mary in Williamsburg and obtained a license to conduct surveys in the county. It was a short course, and by the year 1749, he had his license. Then he reached out to Lord Fairfax regarding his land tracts.

Washington – A Land Surveyor

Lord Fairfax hired George after he obtained his license. Washington, recruited his former mentor, John Genn to assist in the expedition. George, Lord Fairfax, and James Genn set out, first to a valley that the Shenandoah River cut through. "Shenandoah" was a name in the local Native American language meaning "Daughter of the Stars." In the Shenandoah region, they met a number of Native Americans. John Genn could speak their tongue somewhat, and the tribe befriended them. One time, the surveying party even joined in one of the tribal celebrations during which there was a great fire and a lot of dancing. George described it, saying, "…the best dancer jumps about the ring in a most comical manner and is followed by the rest…Then the musicians play music with rattles and a half pot water with deerskin stretched over it which they beat with sticks." That was an 18th-century version of a drum.

In 1752, after completing his task in the Blue Ridge Mountains, Washington secured temporary work for the Ohio Company, which was funded by English land investors who were interested in expanding the British American colonies. The Ohio Company had made an arrangement with five nations of Native Americans to take possession of some parcels of land in the Ohio Valley and planned to establish new colonies there. However, the French also wanted to create their own colonies along the Mississippi and the Ohio River. France already had possession of Louisiana at that time, and new French colonies would represent a northward expansion to the Canadian border. To bolster support, France made arrangements with local tribes there. Washington noted that England and France were reaching a crisis point over control of the area.

Death of His Brother

In the same year, 1752, Washington's stepbrother, Lawrence, developed tuberculosis, which was called "consumption" in those days. For health reasons, George took Lawrence to Barbados, since the warmer climate might help cure him. The journey eased his symptoms but only to a limited degree. Shortly after his return, Lawrence became much more ill, and within three months he died.

After Lawrence died, his widow, Anne, took over the estate at Mount Vernon. She had lifetime rights to the plantation, and upon her death, George was entitled by his father's will to assume ownership. When Anne remarried, she and her new husband moved and leased the property to George. He then moved there, while his mother remained in Fredericksburg.

Shortly after arriving, Washington developed smallpox. Although smallpox claimed many victims, George Washington was strong and survived. He spent time during his recovery sitting on the terrace of the mansion that overlooked the Potomac.

When his brother Lawrence died, it left his position of adjutant of the Virginia Militia open. Washington still had an intense interest in military service, so he lobbied for the post, was accepted, and appointed a major after his training. His mother realized how strongly he wanted this, so she didn't object this time. When it was discovered that George was familiar with the Ohio Valley, he was promoted to lieutenant colonel and sent to the region by General Dinwiddie as a scout to protect the interests of Great Britain. He was given a regiment of troops, which he led into the Ohio Valley.

In the Ohio Valley – 1753

Once Washington reached the Ohio Valley, he made contact with the tribes there as he had done before on his land surveying missions. Just east of the Ohio River, Washington introduced himself to the Seneca tribal chieftain, Tanacharison, a spokesman for the Seneca, Iroquois, and other tribal nations. Tanacharison responded well to this respectful and friendly man, and Washington was able to earn his interest in dealing with the English.

While exploring the mountainous regions in the valley, Washington noted that the French had started building forts in the area, including a huge fort at two tributaries of the Ohio River named Fort Duquesne. Upon his return, Washington reported the information about the

French forts back to Dinwiddie. Dinwiddie then related that to his superiors in England. In the hopes of drawing up an agreement, England told the French that Great Britain also had interests in the Ohio Valley. French officials made numerous excuses and deliberately delayed any proposed meetings. England sent follow-up messages, but those letters were ignored. The crisis was coming to a head.

The French and Indian War

In 1754, Dinwiddie sent Washington back to the Ohio Valley with more troops and orders to expel the French. Washington took the same route he had before and was met by his Native American friend, Tanacharison. Tanacharison warned Washington about a large French military scouting party at a glen east of the Ohio River. In exchange for exclusive trading rights with the British, Tanacharison agreed to rally his warriors in support of Washington.

Washington's forces were relatively small because the British were having difficulty enticing colonies in British America to send militias into the Ohio Valley. Virginia, however, did send some troops (about 150), along with a colonel by the name of Joshua Fry, some British regulars, and a small contingent from the North Carolina Militia. In the meantime, Tanacharison attempted to get the support of more tribes, specifically the Delaware and Shawnee tribes, and he was successful to a limited degree. Washington, his militia, and his new tribal allies started to build a fortification which he called "Fort Necessity." It took a month to construct. During this time, the colonel from Virginia, Joshua Fry, died suddenly from a fall from his horse. Dinwiddie then promoted Washington to full colonel.

Battle of Fort Necessity

Before Washington was able to obtain sufficient supplies and replace his gunpowder, Louis de Jumonville's forces descended on them. Washington's forces were outnumbered by the French and were forced to fight on the open field outside the fort. Washington was also hampered by the poor aim of some of the British regulars assigned to him. After engaging the French, he was forced to retreat back to his fort. Although Washington's men fought courageously, he had to surrender.

However, Washington wasn't familiar with the French language, and the surrender terms indicated that he had "assassinated" Louis' brother at the prior battle at the glen.

When his commanding officer noted the so-called assassination, he questioned Washington. Although Washington explained the error, indicating that Louis de Jumonville's brother died during battle, they were ambivalent about trusting young George Washington. This error disparaged his future reputation. The date was July 3, 1754.

Battle of Fort Duquesne

Great Britain had lost confidence in George Washington due to the translation error. So this time, they sent in Major General Edward Braddock from Great Britain, and appointed him the head of the French and Indian War in British America. Washington was then instructed to join him along with Lieutenant Colonel Thomas Gage at the Monongahela River. Daniel Boone, the famous frontiersman, was among Braddock's troops, having been hired on as a wagoner.

General Braddock was accustomed to the block formations of the British military. Washington advised him against that, indicating that the enemy tribes allied with the French would fight from the woods and shrubbery, rather than in traditional formations. Braddock chose to ignore Washington's advice and set up the troops into rigid formations consisting of two lines and had Colonel Gage split off to his flank. Washington held up the rear guard. Like Washington, Daniel Boone felt that Braddock's formations would make them vulnerable to guerrilla-style tactics.

The French and their tribal allies fired from the woods and forced the British to engage them there. That confused the British so they shot without aiming and even ended up killing some of their own men. Many retreated when they saw the marauding tribesmen, including Boone who was disgusted at the military ignorance displayed by the British.

During the encounter, Braddock was seriously injured, so Washington rode to the head of the remaining troops then rode back and forth in the battlefield and gathered his soldiers together. He also had Braddock and the other wounded men carried away from the battlefield. There weren't enough able-bodied British soldiers left, so that made a counter-attack unfeasible. This was a significant defeat. As for Braddock, he later died of his wounds. The year was 1758.

Operation at Fort Duquesne

Washington couldn't obtain a higher commission in the British military because he didn't get a recommendation from General Braddock before his death. Washington knew the region and he knew the fighting style of the French Canadians and their tribal allies, so he felt frustrated.

Washington and his men were then relegated to work on a road nearby that would give the new British commander, General John Forbes, access to Fort Duquesne in order to attack it again. After a crucial section of the road was finished, Forbes marched towards the fort. However, he neglected to send out scouting parties to gather intelligence, so he was handily defeated by the French before reaching the fort.

Forbes was puzzled when he saw no activity there and asked Washington to inspect it. Washington discovered that the fort was burned by the French after they abandoned it. There was little left of the structure but broken wood and smoldering debris. The tribal warriors had also beheaded some of the British soldiers from Scotland and displayed their kilts above them. Washington had seen that type of brutality before, but many of his soldiers had not and were utterly shocked and disgusted.

Later it was discovered that the French had abandoned the fort for two reasons: 1) their supply lines had been cut, and 2) they had lost the support of the native tribes. So, the French forces made their way toward another fort they held, Fort Legonier.

The British decided to send in some fresh forces to construct a new fort near the site called Fort Pitt, named after the English secretary of state, William Pitt. As for Washington, the British generals still didn't trust him to be in command. He was sent back to Virginia, to be on-call with the Virginia Militia.

From Tranquility to Turmoil

After he left the Ohio Valley area, George returned home to the tranquility of Mount Vernon. He envisioned his future as a Southern planter, earning his living in the agrarian lifestyle among his family and friends. He also associated with the landed gentry of the area and kept pace with current events.

Mount Vernon: Plantation and Manufacturing

The main family crop on the Mount Vernon plantation was tobacco. Unlike other landowners in Virginia, Washington assumed a lot of the duties of management of the plantation and adjoining farm. He rose early, patrolled his estate, and even broke in new horses himself. In addition, he was his own clerk and carefully kept track of the supplies and expenditures needed to run Mount Vernon. In the interest of frugality, he established some manufacturing on site. When he made his rounds, Washington firmly advised his workers that they shouldn't buy anything they could make themselves. There was a blacksmith shop on the premises for the horses, and the blacksmith sold services to neighboring farms as well. Washington also built a small four mill and had a specially fashioned wood-burner built for the making of charcoal to heat the house. Washington employed the services of a number of carpenters whom he hired to frame houses near Alexandria. A staff of weavers produced linen from wool he purchased from England. What they couldn't manufacture at Mount Vernon was ordered from England.

Near the river, Washington had a fishery. In his writings, Washington reported, "This river is well-supplied with various kinds of fish at all seasons of the year...shad, bass, herrings, perch, carp and sturgeon." The staff, as well as Washington and his family, ate fish for their main meals.

Washington's Pre-Revolutionary Military Career

The renown earned by George Washington during the Revolutionary War could lead anyone to assume that Washington had in fact been a graduate of a proper military academy, trained in all the arts of war and leadership. In truth, he learned his military trade through experience rather than education. His earliest experiences proved frustrating and even disastrous, resulting in loss of life, territory and reputation. However, the lessons he learned would enable him to shine later in his life, especially in the pivotal battles he fought during America's war for independence.

First action

George Washington was in his late teens when he took over the militia commission left by the death of his elder brother Lawrence. While in this position, Washington did everything he could to gain recognition in the hopes of obtaining a commission in the regular British Army. His first assignment was as a British military envoy, tasked with delivering a message to the French forces that occupied a portion of the Ohio River Valley. This area was under heavy dispute between the French and the English, and control of it was vital for anyone who wished to claim control of the northern American colonies. Washington delivered the message and gathered valuable intelligence regarding French troop strength and disposition. The message, a demand by the British for the French to retreat from the valley, was rejected, leaving Washington to return home with his volunteer force of about ten men to deliver the bad news.

When they arrived at their destination, Washington's men assisted in the construction of the fort and the defense of the site. Unfortunately, the French, bolstered by their Native American allies, assaulted the site, easily overwhelming and defeating the small British force. Washington was forced to sign a surrender, which claimed he had assassinated the French envoy in his previous encounter. Washington did not fully understand what he was signing as the document was in French and the translation provided was seriously misleading. The admission was used as a propaganda tool for French aggression against the English, and thus became the catalyst that formally began the French and Indian War.

Some accounts suggest that Washington may have influenced Braddock's decision to split his forces in two, thereby weakening his strength and giving the French a chance to defeat him. Others, however, suggest that the defeat was due to the British staff not heeding Washington's advice. In any event, all accounts do agree on the fact that Washington fought with unbridled courage and tenacity. No fewer than two horses were shot out from under him, yet he continued to fight, helping to organize the routed soldiers into an orderly retreat. Such accounts would go on to salvage Washington's military career due to yet another crushing defeat.

Command of Virginian forces

The British government refused to accept responsibility for their defeat by the French, choosing instead to lay the blame solely on the shoulders of Washington himself. This stirred up significant ire amongst the colonials, who were tired of being treated as inferiors by their rulers. As an act of defiance against Britain's efforts to make Washington the scapegoat for their defeat, the colonial authorities made Washington Commander in Chief of all Virginian forces. This position was more important than many people realize today since the Virginian Regiment was the only non-British professional army in the colonies. Thus, Washington became commander of the first true American army.

The primary function of the Virginian Regiment was to protect the frontiers from incursions by the Natives. Washington was successful in achieving this goal, fighting a full twenty battles in only ten months. As a result of the constant fighting Washington lost a full third of his troops, however, the security of the border remained intact, as did Virginia's reputation of being a significant power in the colonies.

His position led to another appointment, this time by General John Forbes, who led another expedition to defeat the French in the Ohio River Valley. Unfortunately, this appointment provided little more than administrative duties, including overseeing the construction of a road that would allow the British forces to march more quickly and safely to their ultimate destination—the French stronghold of Fort Duquesne. Eventually, he was able to participate in some reconnaissance missions, but the only fighting he saw was friendly fire incidents due to inept leadership and a lack of proper intelligence.

Unfortunately, Washington realized that his military prospects would forever be limited to the colonial forces. He subsequently resigned his command of the Virginia Regiment in December of 1758, and would not see military action again until the Revolutionary War.

Washington's Political and Religious Beliefs

Unfortunately, Washington never sat down and wrote anything to formalize his political and religious belief systems. Nevertheless, it is clear that he followed a very precise moral compass in all of his dealings, be they related to business, military, political or family affairs. This moral compass would surface from time to time in correspondence to his younger family members, often in the form of friendly advice. By piecing together the various written documents, contemporary accounts and general behavior of Washington, we can reconstruct a fairly reliable and accurate model of his overall belief system.

View toward freedom

Needless to say, anyone who would risk life and limb fighting for independence would have a very strong belief when it comes to the issue of freedom. However, it's all too easy to take for granted the fact that those fighting for independence would be the victors. The truth of the matter is that victory was never inevitable, especially in light of the military power that England had at her disposal. Fortunately, Washington prized his belief in freedom above any practical concerns regarding the Revolution's chances of success.

Another obstacle that Washington's belief in freedom had to overcome was a sense of loyalty and duty. Again, in modern times it's easy to forget that the people living in mid eighteenth century America were British subjects. In fact, Washington had tried on several occasions to secure a commission in the British army. Fortunately, his efforts were never successful. However, several accounts show an evolution of conscience, one that took Washington from being a staunch loyalist to a fervent supporter of independence. In the end, it seems that freedom was of paramount importance to Washington, overshadowing all other virtues that he came to be respected for.

Religious beliefs

There is no definitive evidence regarding Washington's religious and spiritual beliefs, however, it is easy to imagine what they might have been from the choices he made regarding religion and religious practice. It seems clear that Washington did maintain a certain religious belief system, albeit one that reflected a more intellectual view on life and the world he lived in. While he did attend church on occasion it has been suggested that Washington did not do so frequently. Instead, it seems his time in church was mostly the result of specific celebrations or ceremonies, including weddings, funerals and the like. An account by General Robert Porterfield states that Washington was a pious man who took Communion on a regular basis. Considering the unique nature of this account it seems that it could have been an attempt to paint Washington in a more favorable light within the religious community.

Several quotes attributed to Washington do suggest that he had very strong feelings regarding religious extremism. One particular quote reveals his belief that religious animosity among men is stronger and more dangerous than any other form, and that the world would be a better place if such animosity were completely removed. Still, the way in which Washington incorporated the term "God" in many of his correspondences reflects a man who did have a heartfelt belief in a divine being, one, which engendered respect, reverence and humility.

Perhaps the most important aspect of Washington's religious belief system is the fact that he was highly tolerant of different religions, doctrines and overall world views. Whether this was the result of his passion for philosophy and free thinking, or it had some other cause, we may never truly know. All we can be sure of is that Washington had no room in his heart for religious extremism and the hatred it created among otherwise good and decent human beings.

Role of government

Washington's view on the role of government was highly influential in his choosing to side with the revolutionary cause. While Britain possessed a representative body in the form of Parliament, it was still very much defined as a monarchy. As a result, the role of the king as opposed to the individual was a hotly debated subject. Washington believed that a government should be there to protect the rights of the individual, not to dictate how the individual lived. Furthermore, the policies of government should be determined by the common man, not by someone born into power as a result of royal lineage.

In terms of American government, Washington was very much in favor of a centralized form of government, as opposed to allowing each state to remain largely sovereign and independent. It was his contention that a strong central government could help ensure peace and stability between states, as well as peace and stability with the other nations of the world. That said, Washington was never willing to identify with any one political party. Instead, he resisted being drawn into the tribal political scene, where people supported a candidate for their party rather than their policies. Washington asserted that policies and policies alone should determine the value and capability of a candidate. In essence, Washington could be considered the first Independent politician in American history.

View toward slavery

One of the biggest questions that many grapple with is how a generation of people who were willing to fight and die for freedom were also willing to own slaves. Needless to say, there were many views on slavery at the time, including those that stated slaves were not actual people, as well as those that believed slavery should be abolished altogether. As with his political views, Washington's views on slavery underwent a certain evolution during the course of his lifetime, taking him from one end of the spectrum to the other.

At first, Washington adopted the prevalent view of slavery, namely that it was a natural and proper form of labor. This acceptance of slavery can be easily explained by the fact that he inherited his first slaves at the age of ten. It stands to reason that Washington would simply continue practicing the status quo at such a young age, only starting to question the practice later in life when his world view became more clearly defined.

Fortunately, as time progressed, Washington began to discover that his moral compass did not subscribe to the institution of slavery. In fact, several accounts state that Washington treated his slaves in a very humane way, so much so that they were regarded as part of his family. While he purchased and sold slaves in his earlier years, Washington later found that his heart was staunchly against the practice of treating a human being like a head of livestock. In fact, he wrote at one point that were it not for his distaste of the practice he would like to sell all of his slaves so that he could be done with the practice once and for all. By the time of his death, Washington had found the solution to this crisis. In his last will and testament, he freed upwards of 100 slaves from his estate at Mount Vernon, bequeathing the others to heirs with the hopes that they would be freed later on.

The American Revolution

Although the Continental Congress had begun to enact laws, the country did not have any laws in place to deal with issues that arise during a time of war. Washington, as commander of the colonial forces, agreed that the Congress should be the supreme authority over the army but the army still needed a free rein to some extent. In fact, Washington's commission gave him the power and authority to act in the manner that he felt was in the best interest of the country and the army.

In order to find a workable solution to the issue of having civilian control over the army, it was decided that for major decisions which were not immediate, Washington would present the issue to Congress. If there was an issue where Washington did not have time to consult Congress then he would act as he saw fit and then inform Congress of his actions. If Congress disapproved of Washington's actions, he would be informed of this disapproval and Washington would not repeat them. If Congress remained silent on any issue then this could be interpreted as consent for Washington's actions. This method worked well and Washington ensured that he always informed Congress of his actions when acting on his own and as a result there was never any serious conflict between the two.

Washington came to realize that if the colonies wanted to win the war against Britain, they needed to become independent. As a result, he started encouraging policies that would commit the colonies to independence. This was particularly important because the Continental Congress was split into three factions with each faction favoring a different outcome. One faction led by Samuel Adams, Benjamin Franklin and Richard Henry Lee were in favor of independence and wanted to bring the fight to the British. The second faction, the moderates led by Benjamin Harrison and Robert Morris, wanted the colonies to fight the British in order to conclude a settlement that would address the American issues. This faction was willing to agree to independence but only as a last resort. The third faction within the Continental Congress was led by John Dickinson and wanted to remain a part of the British Empire. This faction hoped to come to some kind of agreement in regards to self-taxation and other issues concerning the colonies.

One of Washington's first steps as the new commander of the military forces was to recommend that the Continental Congress give him enough money so that he could pay his troops to stay in the army for longer periods of time. He also insisted that the British commander of Boston was required to treat captured American officers as prisoners of war and not as rebels. He even attempted to persuade colonists in Canada to join America in its revolution against King George. In addition to these actions, Washington also helped develop a small six vessel navy that could be used to attack British ships attempting to bring supplies into Boston.

Washington's first success in the war against Britain occurred in Boston, where he forced the British troops to withdraw from the city. Washington's navy fleet was able to intercept supplies from Britain and he was able to keep the city under siege for over eight months. He had a number of cannons that were captured from Fort Ticonderoga placed on high points overlooking the city. This gave Washington the ability to direct cannon fire into the British encampment. The British, recognizing their tactical disadvantage, were forced to withdraw from the city by way of the sea.

Washington's success in taking Boston further enhanced his reputation and helped sustain the confidence of the American public. This victory also helped give the colonies confidence to sign the Declaration of Independence on July 4, 1776.

A few days after the signing of the Declaration of Independence, the British launched an attack on New York. The capture of New York would give the British a number of advantages in the war. It would be a propaganda victory since the British would be in control of the largest city in the colonies. It would also give the British access to a deep water port and the Hudson River which could be used to move British troops into the interior of America to fight the colonists.

Britain launched the attack by landing thirty thousand troops on Staten Island and in August, these thirty thousand troops attacked the colonial forces. The colonial forces either surrendered or ran away. When the British landed on Manhattan, the colonial forces once again ran away from the advancing British troops. Washington was enraged by the actions of the colonial forces.

Washington recognized that if he hoped to win the war he would need to change his tactics. He would have to stop attempting to engage the British in open fields with standard firing lines and instead he would need to adopt the tactics of the Native Americans that had been so successful during the French and Indian War. On Christmas Day, 1776, Washington and his troops surprised the British stationed at Trenton. Washington followed up this success with an attack on a British garrison in Princeton a few days later. Although these victories were only minor and did not constitute full-fledged battles, they did serve to give a boost to morale for the Americans as well as letting the British know that the Americans have not giving up their efforts to gain independence.

The turning point for the American Revolution occurred in its third year when Major General Horatio Gates won the battle at Saratoga. British general, John Burgoyne, attempted an invasion by leading his army south into the American colonies from Quebec. Burgoyne hoped to isolate New England but another British general, William Howe, sent his army which was stationed in New York to Philadelphia instead of moving north to join with Burgoyne. Burgoyne ended up trapped and had to surrender his army at Saratoga.

This was a major victory for the American colonials and helped to convince the French that the Americans could win the war. The French began to look more favorably on the possibility of an alliance between the two countries as a way to gain some of the goods that were being taken in the raids on British ships as well as antagonize their old enemy England.

Although America enjoyed some victories in the war, Washington did not have as much luck. He was defeated in two major battles during 1777 and was unable to stop the British from taking the town of Philadelphia when General Howe moved his army south to attack the town. Philadelphia was the seat of the American government at this time and the government was forced to go into hiding. Some members of

Congress attempted to replace Washington as commander as a result of these losses but this attempt was not successful as Washington's supporters rallied behind him.

During the winter of 1777 – 1778, Washington and his troops had to endure freezing conditions at Valley Forge. Once winter was over, the American army was able to train and become a better fighting force which was then in a better position to fight the British. The French also entered into an alliance with the American forces in May 1778 and by 1779, France had sent six thousand soldiers to help fight the British and strengthen the colonial army.

In 1778, the British made the decision to invade the southern colonies. The British hoped that they would be able to conquer the southern colonies and then take a large consolidated army back up north to drive out the colonial rebels. Although the British were initially successful and able to conquer both Savannah, Georgia in 1778 and Charleston, South Carolina in 1779, they found themselves having to face the guerrilla war tactics of the American colonials. The colonials refused to stand and fight and would simply melt into the forest or countryside after an attack. The British had to face American sharpshooters who would attack the British and then simply disappear into the forest.

In addition to the American sharpshooters, the Americans had other advantages when it came to fighting the British. One advantage was that most colonials could attack on their own and could move much faster than the British soldiers since they were not weighed down with large amounts of equipment. Another advantage had to do with distance. British soldiers who were needed to replace casualties had to be sent from England on a trip that could last for several weeks. The colonials kept up their attacks, wearing down the British army and by 1781, most of the British population were strongly against the war in America.

In the summer of 1781, Washington was informed that the British southern force was situated in Chesapeake Bay in Virginia so Washington began to secretly move his army towards Chesapeake Bay. He was able to utilize counterintelligence techniques to confuse the British and keep them in the dark about his true objective. While Washington's army was moving towards the British army, commanded by Lord Cornwallis, the French were sailing their fleet from the West Indies to the Virginia coast.

On September 1, 1781, the French fleet arrived off the Virginia coast and were able to form a blockade, which would block the British from being able to retreat by sea from the approaching American army. Three days later, on September 4, 1781, Washington's combined force made up of American and French soldiers arrived and began to bombard the British forces in the town of Yorktown. There was an attempt on September 5 by the British Navy to evacuate British troops but the French fleet was able to fight the British ships off, leaving Cornwallis's soldiers to their fate.

Washington continued to bombard the town for over two weeks as well as launching infantry charges to overrun the British positions. By October 16, 1781, Cornwallis, after a meeting with his senior officers, who all agreed they were in a hopeless situation, decided to surrender. The surrender was signed on October 19, 1781.

Washington didn't know it at the time, but Yorktown was the last hostile engagement between the two combatants. The British still had a number of soldiers in America and the French had left leaving the American's to deal with any further hostilities on their own. Washington not only had to deal with the possibility of a continuing British attack but he also had to deal with his own men who were becoming increasingly upset over the fact that they had not been paid for some time.

There was even talk about a **coup d'état** but Washington was able to diffuse the situation by meeting with the officers of the army and giving an emotional speech which asked for patience, and for all army officers to oppose any military action against Congress. Most of the officers present had been working closely with Washington for a number of years and as a result, were willing to put an end to any talk of possible military action against Congress. To help diffuse the situation, Congress also agreed to pay some of the money owed to the army as well as pay each soldier five years worth of full pay.

The British were tired of the war by this time and were no longer willing to continue fighting. They entered into peace negotiations with the

Americans in April, 1783 which resulted in the Treaty of Paris being signed on September 3, 1783. This treaty was negotiated by Benjamin Franklin, John Hay, Henry Laurens and John Adams for the Americans and David Hartley and Richard Oswald for the British. The treaty ended the war between England and America and was ratified by the American congress on January 4, 1784.

Once Britain agreed to recognize America's independence, Washington disbanded the colonial army on November 2, 1783 and on November 25, the British left New York City. Washington then resigned as the commander of the colonial forces on December 23, 1783 much to the amazement of the nobility in Europe who expected that Washington would take over power. King George III described Washington as **"the greatest character of the age"** because of Washington's willingness to resign his commission. After Washington resigned his commission he went back to his home in Mount Vernon to attempt to restore his property which had deteriorated while he fought the British.

REVOLUTION STRIKES: THE BATTLE FOR DEMOCRACY

Washington himself yearned to be a part of His Majesty's military. As a teenager he dreamed of being in the Royal Navy, and during his own military career he wanted to be a part of the Crown's command. But over time he would begin to value a strong national government over sovereignty from a ruler that was an ocean away.

The following chapter will examine the rise of Washington as a key character of the American Revolution, and chart the new set of values shared by the colonists that would forge the separation of the colonies from British rule.

Dissidence Strikes: The Stamp Act of 1765

In 1765 a simple vote by the British Parliament would begin widespread dissidence throughout the American colonies. The Stamp Act was a direct tax placed on the colonies which required that any printed materials—newspapers, magazines, legal documents, etc.—had to be printed on paper that was manufactured and 'stamped' in London. The tax would have to be paid in British currency rather than American currency. The act was immediately extremely unpopular amongst the colonists that considered the measure a direct violation of their rights as Englishmen to be taxed without consent. The British Parliament argued that the tax was meant to pay for the British military men leftover in the Americas following the French-Indian war. The Americans countered that the British military was no longer needed, and the expense should be picked up by the British.

As stated in previous chapters, American colonists did not generally dislike the British. As evidenced by Washington himself, many idealized and wanted to be a part of British rule in America. This was until the will of the British began trumping the rights and sovereignty of the American people, and the American people acted swiftly, violently, and without fear of recourse.

Colonialists began to prepare petitions and arrange protests across the colonies. The Stamp Act Congress was held in New York City and was the first time that colonies joined together in protest of a British law. A coalition was founded that united New England colonies all the way to Maryland and organized protests and demonstrations. The Sons of Liberty—which would later become famous during the Revolution—was founded and often turned demonstrations into violent affairs.

Quickly, the businessmen responsible for the sale of stamp taxed products were too intimidated and the tax itself was never properly collected. Opposition became so fierce in the colonies that it spread to Britain, where merchants and manufacturers feared retribution on their products. The Stamp Act was eventually repealed, but the British put forth similar measures to demonstrate their power that would continue to aggravate the colonists.

Washington Joins the Revolution

Washington voiced his opposition to the Stamp Act but it wasn't until the Townshend Acts in 1767 that he began to take a more active role in colonial resistance. The Townshend Act took a different approach to collecting taxes. Rather than collecting direct taxes—like with the failed Stamp Act—the Townshend Act would take indirect taxes in the form of taxed imports. Imports such as tea, glass, and paint, which could not be produced in America, were among the newly taxed products. The colonies saw through the new plan and protested as they had previously.

Washington and his friend George Mason put together a proposal that would result in the boycotting of all English goods until the Townshend Act was lifted. The act was eventually repealed, but new laws were put in place that limited the rights to self-government in some colonies, particularly Massachusetts following the Boston Tea Party when colonists dumped a large shipment of tea into Boston Harbor. With every protest and repeal, the British followed up with a new tactic that replaced one form of tyranny with another.

Washington's success in helping repeal the Townshend Act prompted him to help organize the First Continental Congress. The

First Continental Congress was held in Philadelphia with 56 delegates from 12 of the 13 colonies. This was an enormously important movement in the lead up to the Revolutionary War as it was the first instance, besides the organized protests of various British resolutions that the colonies united to air grievances against Britain. The result of the Congress was a boycott against all British goods and the threat to halt exports to Britain if Parliament didn't lift bans made in Massachusetts.

War Erupts: 1775-1783

Following restrictive laws placed on Massachusetts in reaction to the Boston Tea Party, a parallel 'rebel' government was formed by the colonists to govern the colony outside of the British ruled Boston. The British considered this to be a 'rebel colony' and attacked local militia in Lexington and Concord. With these attacks, the American Revolution began, and war between the colonies and the British Empire began.

Under Washington's suggestion, a Second Continental Congress was called in Philadelphia where Washington attended in full military uniform. While the First Congress set out to mend relations with Britain, the Second Congress decided to respond to the attacks and plan for independence.

The Declaration of Independence was signed, military actions were strategized, diplomats and formal treaties were created, and the delegates present at the Congress became a de facto government of the 13 colonies. Washington was named the Commander-in-Chief and was put in charge of building, organizing, and training a new national army.

Washington carefully chose the men that would lead alongside him, and although they would lose many battles to the British, adopted the strategy of keeping his men in the field ready to fight at all times. Just as he had learned hard discipline through years of farming, surveying, and soldiering, he convinced the not yet formed nation to give up support of untrainable militias for a highly trained professional and unified army. Washington became known for his large scale battles against the British. Throughout the war that lasted 8 years, Washington would also use strategic tactics to oust the Native Americans that had allied with the

British and use the French army—which he had fought against previously—to fight against the British.

The Treaty of Paris in 1783 had Great Britain formally recognize the independence of the newly formed United States of America. Washington disbanded the army and resigned as Commander in Chief soon thereafter—he was heralded worldwide, including by King George III himself for immediately relinquishing power of the Army.

The Man for the People: Soldier, Politician, Leader

Although he did not even want to attend, Washington was elected as President of the Constitutional Convention in 1787. He encouraged a strong central government as necessary to support a brand new nation. Washington was widely popular, both among his fellow delegates and the people for his wide set of accomplishments. When the Constitution was finally ratified, the Presidency of the new nation was developed with Washington in mind and with the idea to allow him precedent in defining the role of President once he was elected.

What were the characteristics of George Washington that gave him such precedent, and how can those characteristics be repeated in today's leadership to create a truer upholding of democracy?

Strong core values: honesty, integrity, personal responsibility

Fight for the common good vs. Individual desires

Courage in the face of great challenge

Unwavering belief in individual freedoms and sovereignty

Willingness to fight for one's core beliefs and freedoms

After the War

Once the war had ended, a number of problems arose as the various states within America began to look after their own interests, and not those of the country as a whole. For example, Rhode Island began imposing taxes on traffic that passed through the state and Virginia and Maryland began to argue over the Potomac River and where the boundary for each state should be set.

Other difficulties faced by the States included the fact that there were not enough markets abroad for American goods which forced the Americans to either buy products with money instead of trade or to buy items on credit. The British also refused to allow American ships access to the British West Indies to trade.

In addition to these difficulties, there was a money shortage which made it difficult for people to pay their bills. Congress and the states also had difficulty paying back the debts they had incurred in order to finance the war. Debtors began to demand that more money be printed so that they could use this money to pay off their debts. A number of states decided to do this but it had a negative effect on creditors since the currency depreciated as a result of simply printing more money. The dispute between debtors and creditors resulted in an uprising which threatened to cause the downfall of the state government of Massachusetts.

The problems being faced by the newly independent country were partly blamed on the weak central government that had been established by the Articles of Confederation. The Articles of Confederation had been approved by the Continental Congress to establish the country of America and give Congress the power to conduct the war with England.

The Articles of Confederation did not allow the central government to have a single currency since money issues were controlled by the states. The Articles also did not allow Congress to levy taxes so it could not pay for a standing army or raise enough money to pay off what Congress had borrowed.

Washington was concerned by the weak central government and wanted a strong government to help protect property, allow a country wide currency to be developed and to protect creditors from state laws which would have a negative effect on them. Washington also wanted a strong central government that could levy taxes in order to pay off the national debt and have enough money to run the country. He also thought that a central government could help develop domestic production of manufactured goods and lessen America's dependence on foreign products.

A meeting of all thirteen states was held in May 1787 in the city of Philadelphia. The point of this meeting, which became known as the Constitutional Convention, was to develop a new system of government. Washington was elected the leader of this convention and it was his leadership abilities that helped convince the states to ratify the new constitution. The new constitution called for the new government to have three branches in order to help ensure that no one group would be able to exert undue influence over the government as a whole. The new constitution gave the government the power to deal with issues that affected the country as a whole while still leaving the states in control of a number of issues such as schools, family relations and non-federal crimes. The constitution also called for a president to be elected to lead the country.

Once the new constitution had been passed, the country began to look for a person who had the personality and ability to hold the new office of president. Most people automatically turned to Washington as the best man to lead the new country. Washington was reluctant to become the new president and the first presidential election was more an attempt to convince Washington to run than it was to choose between the various candidates. People wrote a number of letters trying to convince Washington to stand for the presidency. Many of the letters stated that his country needed him and that he did not have a good reason for refusing. Washington slowly began to accept the idea of becoming president.

Washington finally agreed to run for president and as per the new constitution, the president was chosen by the Electoral College. The way in which people were selected to be part of the Electoral College was up to the state legislature. This meant that in some states, an election was held and in others, people were chosen by the legislature. Three of the thirteen states did not participate in the first presidential election because two of them, Rhode Island and North Carolina, had not ratified the constitution in time for the election and the third state, New York, did not choose its Electoral College members in time.

Each member of the Electoral College had two votes to cast for president. Every member cast one of their votes for Washington and he is the only president to ever receive unanimous support from the Electoral College. The person with the second highest amount of votes was John Adams who was named vice president.

Washington only wanted to serve one term as president but he reluctantly agreed to stand for a second term because he saw that there was still a lot to do in order to ensure the success of the new country. His decision to run a second time was partly influenced by the growing conflict between Alexander Hamilton, the Secretary of the Treasury, and Thomas Jefferson, the Secretary of State. Washington was worried that if he left, the growing division between the two men and their backers would cause the country to fall apart. He was also worried about America's involvement in foreign affairs. In the second election, Washington was again voted in unanimously. He could also have served a third term if he wished since it was a given that if he ran he would be elected again. Washington refused the third time and turned over responsibility to John Adams, his vice-president. Washington's example of only running two times was followed for approximately one hundred and fifty years until Franklin Roosevelt was elected to a third and fourth term.

The Constitutional Convention

George Washington's peaceful life at Mount Vernon was short-lived, he was soon pulled back into the nation's affairs when he started to realize that the nation's Articles of Confederation were not functioning as planned. By 1787, the union between the states was crumbling under the current Articles of Confederation, and George realized a new form of government was needed as the union was becoming weaker and weaker. Under the Articles of Confederation, the union was unable to pay debts or collect revenue along with appalling diplomatic and military leadership by the Confederation Congress. Since gaining independence, the young nation was struggling to work with a structure of government that centered power with the states.

Because the states were not unified, this power structure was messy as they fought over boundaries, navigation rights, and who would pay off the nation's debt from the Revolutionary War. There were even some state legislatures that resorted to unethical means by imposing oppressive and dictatorial tax policies on their very own citizens! George knew a solid reform was vital, but he was not sure if making democratic adjustments so soon after the Revolution was the best timing. That was until Shays' rebellion exploded in Massachusetts.

Although George Washington was compensated handsomely after the Revolutionary War, other farmers who risked their lives fighting received very little compensation for their efforts. Many of them were struggling terribly in the 1780s and could hardly make ends meet for their families. Paper money was all but out of circulation and because these farmers had no access to gold and silver, Boston's businesses were no longer accepting credit or barter for the goods farmers needed. Instead, they were demanding immediate payments, payments many farmers didn't have. These issues, coupled with Massachusetts residents who were paying higher taxes than ever before, made it all but impossible for farmers to move their crops and make money. Boston authorities began arresting farmers and foreclosing on their farms.

When a peaceful settlement attempt by the farmers failed, Shays' Rebellion in 1786 was a string of violent attacks on courthouses and other government locations in Massachusetts by ex-Revolutionary War soldiers turned farmers. The rebellion came to a violent head in 1787 when Daniel Shays, an ex-solider after whom the rebellion was named, and more than a thousand men armed with guns, clubs, and pitchforks, came head to head with a military arsenal.

Although many of the rebels were later pardoned for their actions by Governor John Hancock, this rebellion was a strong indicator that the Articles of Confederation were too weak to effectively manage the newly-formed United States. George Washington saw this predicament, and he knew that Shays' Rebellion illustrated how something needed to be done to vastly improve his nation's current governmental structure. In fact, he was so disheartened with the current state of affairs that he decided to write to James Madison, a founding father and later America's fourth president, to start the process of creating what we know today to be the American Constitution. In 1786, Congress approved a convention, to be held in Philadelphia the following year, to amend the Articles of Confederation.

In 1787, George Washington again left his life at Mount Vernon and became a leading mover towards reform when he joined the Constitutional Convention in Philadelphia to recommend changes to the Articles of Confederation. Washington was unanimously chosen to lead the Constitutional Convention, and for the next four months the men deliberated on how to revise or replace the Articles of Confederation. Washington barely spoke a single word during the convention, yet he lobbied strongly with his fellow delegates to not revise the amendments, but instead create a new constitution. Washington knew that they needed a new plan for their government that would address their nation's current problems as well as future ones. The consensus developed an entirely new plan for their government – the United States Constitution.

Ratifying the Constitution was not easy, as there was harsh opposition from many of America's leading political figures, such as Sam Adams and Patrick Henry (famous for his "Give me liberty, or give me death!" speech), who criticized the document as giving the government too much power. Patrick Henry in particular wrote numerous Anti-

Federalist Papers opposing the United States Constitution. Although these papers were unable to stop the Constitution from being ratified, they were very influential in helping to shape the later Bill of Rights, which are the first ten Amendments to the Constitution.

Washington's own state of Virginia only ratified the Constitution by one vote. But, it was George Washington's stellar reputation that helped overcome this opposition. He worked tirelessly for months to gather support for the ratification of his proposed Constitution and his rallying paid off when the United States Constitution was officially ratified by the states in 1788. With a new Constitution ratified, George Washington was again ready to retire back to Mount Vernon and continue his life in privacy. However, this again would not be in the cards for George. When the first presidential election was held at the end of 1788, Washington was unanimously chosen president by the Electoral College. George receive a vote from every elector, the only president to this day to be elected by a unanimous vote. George Washington was now 57-years-old.

Impact

Political

In the years following the end of George Washington's terms as president, the political and economic face of the United States continued to bear his mark. The divisions that had emerged during his two terms between supporters of the political vision of Alexander Hamilton and those who favored Thomas Jefferson grew further under the presidency of John Adams (1797-1801). Although, like his predecessor, he attempted to govern beyond the partisan struggles, his international policy favored Jeffersonian views. With George Washington failing to maintain his apolitical perception of government, it was under his presidency that bipartisanship was born, which would mark the coming centuries: the Federalists inspired the future Republican Party, while the Republican Democrats would be at the origin of the Democratic Party.

Meanwhile, the economy was deeply anchored in the industrialization of the north and finance. Promoting the emergence of a new economy based on industry and stock exchanges, George Washington was also launching the great adventure of American banking, both public and private, which was not particularly successful. The first federal bank was replaced by a second in 1812, but until 1863, the issuing of currency was not registered. However, the National Bank Act of that year limited the issuance of currency to private banks, whose bills could be charged as federal pension assets. In 1913, the Federal Reserve endorsed the monopoly of issuance of the federal government.

The American Civil War and the conquest of the West

In the southern states in the 1790s, the challenges of the future American Civil War (1861-1865) emerged. Indeed, the agricultural and planting economy was growing. While it was initially based on the cultivation of tobacco, technical innovations in spinning and the rise in demand favored the cultivation of cotton, which quickly spread. This culture, which required a significant work force, was mainly operated by slaves whose population was growing: in the second half of the

18th century, they accounted for between one sixth and one third of the total population of the United States. With the advance westward, the newly conquered lands were vested in the cultivation of tobacco, cotton and dye plants, which resulted in the displacement of enslaved populations. From the 1770s, several northern states voted for the abolition of slavery, but George Washington, himself a slave owner who nevertheless repeatedly showed abolitionist inclinations, did not make a decision on the subject. He thus left his successors to tackle this thorny issue, which would be settled at the price of a bloody civil war.

It was also under the presidency of George Washington that the great conquest of the West began, the foundation of the American identity. The first agreements with the Native Americans and the Spaniards, obtained by force or through diplomacy, opened the era of pioneers who sought, through the discovery and conquering of new territories in the West, to extend the political, but above all the economic and commercial influence of the young federal nation.

American Progress by John Gast, 1872. This painting represents the Manifest Destiny, showing that American Settlers were destined to move though the continent.

A solid constitution

Finally, George Washington established the constitutional foundations of the nation, which would still be going strong two centuries later, through the Constitution on which he worked and the amendments that still govern justice and American liberties today. Thanks to a certain idea of diplomacy and the position of the United States on the world stage, which would only really be challenged with the Second World War – during which the United States broke their isolation.

George Washington was also the one who gave the presidential office its meaning. The representation of the role, duties and position of the head of the federal government was largely inherited from his actions. It was under his presidency that the tradition of the president choosing the cabinet himself was born, as was the limitation of the exercise of supreme power to two terms and the appointment of a large number of staff by the head of state (ambassadors, judges of the Supreme Court, etc.). While firmly anchoring the executive power represented by the presidential office, he clearly defined the role of the Congress and its legislative power. He was careful to avoid interfering in debates, except in constitutional matters, and did not use his veto power to influence decisions. During the Whiskey Revolt of 1794, he also demonstrated the superiority of federal power over the states, a power that was at first ensured in a rudimentary manner by armed militias, and whose specificity and functions would be developed in the decades that followed.

The Mansions of Rest 1797-1799

Mount Vernon At Last

"Grandpapa is very well, and has already turned farmer again."

From a letter written by Nelly Custis

George Washington returned to Mount Vernon accompanied by his wife Martha, his granddaughter Nelly Custis, and by George Washington Lafayette and his tutor, as well as Martha's pet dog and Nelly's pet parrot. George and Martha were both elated and relieved to be returning to their home at last. The Washington's had their work cut out for them back at Mount Vernon; just as when George had returned home from the war, he found that the house and the farms had sunk into great disrepair, and needed many expensive repairs. And for Martha's part, the same steady stream of visitors, gawkers, veterans, and old friends that had appeared on their door stop to lay eyes on the old General soon presented themselves in order to catch a glimpse of the retired President. But these were cares and troubles that the Washington's were happy to exchange for the cares and troubles of George's military and political career.

The Quasi War

No sooner had John Adams become president than diplomatic relations between the United States and France abruptly worsened. American ships in the Atlantic were not only being harassed by the British, who were impressing their sailors; French ships also were using the war with Britain as an excuse to board American ships and steal any cargo deemed to be British in origin. Adams sent a diplomatic envoy of three American politicians to France to negotiate the situation with the republican government. The diplomats were not permitted to meet with Talleyrand, the French foreign minister, until they had both paid a personal bribe to Talleyrand and offered a cash loan to France, which they refused to do.

Adams responded by making the United States ready for a potential war: he created a provisional army of 10,000 men and founded the American navy. And because Adams had no real experience in military matters, he wished to give control of the army to Washington, who had more military experience than anyone else. Through an intermediary, Washington expressed that he would be willing to take charge of the army under two conditions: one, that he would not have to leave Mount Vernon and take the field to prepare the armies himself unless the threatened war with France actually broke out, and two, that he be permitted to choose his own generals, men whom he trusted to get the army into an adequate state of readiness without relying on his direct supervision.

Washington had been following the rise of French-American hostilities closely since leaving office. When Lafayette wrote to him with news of his release in 1798, and a proposal to move to Virginia and buy a farm near Mount Vernon, Washington was forced to write back and tell him that there was so much anti-French feeling in the country just then that he was unlikely to find much of a welcome in the United States. Whatever his feelings for Lafayette, Washington was incensed by the behavior of the French, and of the Republicans in Congress who continued to favor France. Feeling that the country needed him, he was once more unable to turn down the call of duty; however, he was considerably taken aback when Adams announced his appointment as commander in chief to the newspapers without writing to ask or confirm his acceptance.

Washington had sent word to Adams, through an intermediary, that he wanted Hamilton for his second in command; of all his subordinates from the war, it was Hamilton he trusted to prepare the army as he would wish them prepared. Adams, however, had an intense personal dislike for Hamilton and at first refused to agree to name him to such a high rank, though eventually he conceded. However, the provisional army would be disbanded within two years, as ongoing diplomatic relations with France diminished popular support for war.

Washington's Will
Washington continued to take an eager interest in political affairs—the post arrived three times a week, with bulging bags full of letters and newspapers and pamphlets to keep him up to date. His antipathy to Jefferson and the Republicans had only intensified over time, and he made a point of advising government figures like Hamilton, not to preserve unity, as he had urged during his own administration, but to keep a sharp eye on those who would seek to destabilize the new government through Republican political agendas.

But it was domestic matters that took up the chief part of his time and attention in the last year of his life. With his financial situation worsening, Washington began to consider ways to disentangle himself from slavery in a way that would satisfy his conscience without jeopardizing his farm. Like many of the Founders, Washington had come to develop an intense intellectual revulsion for slavery over the decades, but when challenged by committed abolitionists like Lafayette to take serious strides towards dismantling the system, Washington had always balked. His fear of antagonizing slave owning southern politicians whose cooperation he needed had restrained him, as well as his fear that granting freedom to any of his slaves, or allowing them to mingle with free blacks, would antagonize the others, had made a moral coward out of him in this as in no other aspect of his life. But as he grew older, Washington grew increasingly eager to, as historian Ron Chernow puts it, "free himself of the burden of keeping other human beings in bondage."

The famous provision of Washington's will, ordering the freedom of his slaves at his death, was the result. Completed in July of 1799, only five months before his death, the will was twenty nine pages long. Washington composed it in the utmost secrecy, without consulting a lawyer. Interestingly, even after drafting this will, he kept the copy of the will he made in 1775 before taking command of the Continental army. Hours before his death, he had both wills brought to him in bed, and ordered the 1775 copy burned before his eyes; it has been speculated that this was because he feared that his relatives would seize on any excuse not to carry out his orders regarding his slaves, or else that he himself had not absolutely made up his mind to commit to their freedom until he lay on his death bed.

Only about half of the slaves at Mount Vernon were Washington's to free if he chose. The other half were entailed in the Custis estate that Martha had inherited from her first husband, and would legally pass to Martha's grandson George Washington Custis when she died. Since many of Washington's slaves were married to the dower slaves, Washington knew they would be forced into a painful dilemma, and his unwillingness to deal with that situation prevented him from releasing them during his lifetime. Sensible of the fact that slaves who were given freedom suddenly would have difficulty making their way in the world, Washington set aside funds in his will to feed and house the children and the elderly, and made provisions for the children to be taught to read and write and taught a trade so that they could earn a living. Only one of his slaves, Billy Lee, the valet who was by his side at every moment of the Revolutionary War, was freed and given a pension at the time of Washington's death.

Washington's will was published in pamphlet form and circulated around the country after his death. His decision to free his slaves was extraordinary for a wealthy plantation owner of his era and social class; it was, in fact, as revolutionary a thing as he had ever done. Many of the Founders were abolitionists in name, but even the most committed ones, such as Alexander Hamilton, put their political goals ahead of their principles—and the abolition of slavery was never politically expedient in their lifetimes. Furthermore, as a poor immigrant to America who married into a wealthy northern family, a person such as Hamilton wasn't in a financial situation that made him dependent on slavery; taking an abolitionist stance posed little personal risk to him. This was also true of most of the Founders who opposed slavery in name. While freeing his slaves after his death could not erase the fact that he had held hundreds of human beings in bondage and profited off their labor over the course of his lifetime, the fact remains that Washington's slave owning peers, such as Madison and Jefferson, would never have dreamed of taking such a measure.

In the end, the slaves freed in Washington's will did not have to wait until Martha Washington's death for their release. After a fire at Mount Vernon, which she suspected of having been set by slaves who wished to hasten their freedom by killing her, Martha freed all the Washington slaves a year after her husband's death.

The Death of George Washington

"Washington died in a manner that befit his life: with grace, dignity, self-possession, and a manifest regard for others. He never yielded to shrieks, hysteria, or unseemly complaints... Washington's final hours must have been hellish, yet he endured them with exemplary composure."
Excerpt, **Washington: A Life,** by Ron Chernow

Washington's lifelong habit, whenever he was at Mount Vernon, was to make a daily circuit on horseback of all the farms that comprised his estate. This took him from just after breakfast until about three or four in the afternoon. It was how he gave his personal attention to all of the operations that kept Mount Vernon running, and in his younger days he relished the exercise and activity afforded by the daily ride. By 1799, however, he was sixty eight years old, worn down by the strain of his political career, and not as sure on horseback as he used to be. He began to rely on younger men to help oversee Mount Vernon, but made the ride whenever possible.

On December 12, 1799, Washington made his daily ride of Mount Vernon's farms despite bitterly cold winds, sleet, and snow. When he returned for the mid-day meal, there were guests waiting to eat; rather than forcing them to wait on him, he chose to go straight to dinner without first changing out of his snow-damp clothing. Later that day he began to complain of a sore throat, but the next morning, he went about his work outdoors as usual. By the evening of the thirteenth, his throat was so sore that he could barely speak.

Around two o'clock in the morning of December 14, Washington woke up in severe pain, having difficulty breathing. Modern medical experts suspect that the cause was due to an infection of the epiglottis, which would explain why he choked when he attempted to swallow and had such difficulty breathing and speaking. Martha wanted to send for a doctor immediately, but he refused to let her get out of bed, as she had only just got over a cold. When a slave named Caroline came in to light the fires a few hours later, the best doctors in the area were summoned to Washington's bed side, including Dr. James Craik, who had served with Washington in the French and Indian War.

In their desperation to save him, Washington's three doctors subjected him to the best medical practices known to eighteenth century medicine: blisters, enemas, induced vomiting, and bleeding. It is estimated that over half of Washington's blood was drained. By 4:30 in the afternoon of December 14, Washington knew that he could not survive much longer, and asked Martha to bring him the two wills in his desk; the 1775 version, he asked her to burn, and gave into her hands the one with the provision for the freedom of the slaves. Washington spoke calmly and comfortingly to the doctors and friends who surrounded his bed, declaring that he was not afraid to die, and thanking them for their help.

Washington died around ten o'clock at night on December 14, 1799. According to his instructions, his body was not interred in the vault at Mount Vernon until he had been dead for three days; the precaution, not uncommon in that age, was to prevent premature burial. He was buried on December 18, and his funeral oration was delivered by Henry Lee, his longtime friend and colleague. Martha Washington did not attend; she lived quietly with her grandson in a small set of rooms in the attic of the Mount Vernon mansion house, sewing and occasionally receiving visitors. She died in 1802.

Conclusion

The reason that we still remember Washington so fondly at this point in history is probably due to the fact that, whatever his failings and vulnerabilities, he had a strong desire to always do what was right: for this reason, his contemporaries considered him a trustworthy steward of power, which is nearly the highest approbation that politicians are capable of.

Historians agree that Washington, though by no means incompetent as the general of the Continental army, was not an extraordinarily talented military strategist; it is well known that he lost more battles than he won. His gift was his astonishing ability to keep the army together in the face of incredible odds—to inspire men who were dropping dead of disease, exposure, and starvation, who were not receiving pay, and who did not even have clothes to wear, to keep fighting for eight years until their independence was won. Few leaders with that kind of charisma, who are capable of inspiring that kind of loyalty from an army, would dream of voluntarily giving up that army after the war. No one in the history of European politics had done it. But Washington believed strongly in an idea of what America could be: a self-ruled republic in which power was transferred peacefully from one servant of the people to the next. Even today, the peaceful transfer of power is still considered one of the most distinctive and original characteristics of American democracy.

It is difficult to grasp, from our modern perspective, just how fragile America was at the end of the Revolutionary War, or how much opportunity there was for the early republic to miscarry. A new nation had been created, but no one was in charge of it. If George Washington had not been such a blatantly obvious candidate for the position of the country's first head of state, if he had not been considered so universally trustworthy, and if he had not been so absolutely committed to doing his duty with no thought for the money or power he could have extorted from his position, it is difficult to say what the result might have been. Unity has never been the defining feature of politics in the United States of America—except in the first few years of its existence, when everyone decided to put George Washington in charge. The unprecedented unity he inspired was absolutely necessary in order for the country to define itself, resist the interference of foreign powers, and design a system of government that would endure for generations to come.

When one considers the difficulties that faced the country at its inception, the mythology that sprang up around George Washington, beginning immediately after his death, seems almost understandable: the obstacles he faced were so monumental that it is tempting to believe that only a person who was more than human could have overcome them.

Shortly after Washington's death, a biography of him was written and published by Parson Weems, an Episcopal minister who had made a career of cranking out poorly researched books. He was the originator of the stories about Washington chopping down a cherry tree as a boy, flinging a coin across the Rappahannock River, and beseeching God on his knees for the lives of his soldiers at Valley Forge. Other biographers, though less inclined to make up stories from thin air, did not tend to write about Washington's foibles or quirks, his vulnerabilities, his humor, or his weaknesses. For this reason, the image of Washington that was handed down to posterity was encased in marble, metaphorically speaking, long before the Washington monument was built.

One of the greatest losses that we suffer from having only this soft focus image of Washington transmitted to us is that even though Washington's blessing or disapproval is often invoked by modern politicians for their own agendas, Americans lack a strong cultural understanding of what the father of their country stood for. He worked hard to create the image of a strong leader who rose above factionalism and partisan divisions, but internally, he came to be a committed Federalist who strongly opposed the small government, slave holding, state's rights viewpoints of Jefferson and Madison's Republican Party. He believed in taxes, non-interventionist foreign policy, and strong central government. Rarely are these things mentioned in connection with him today.

In regarding Washington as a paragon or a saint, we also lose the sense that extraordinary deeds are accomplished by ordinary people. It is less inspiring to believe that there has never been a person like Washington before or since in all of history than it is to remember that Washington wanted to be remembered. He did not want power for venal reasons, but he did want to improve upon the circumstances into which he was born and rise above his station. In other words, Washington was not born a hero—but he became one because he worked hard, from the time he was a boy, to make himself into a person with useful skills, a finely honed sense of courtesy towards others, a deep sense of duty, and an eye for opportunities to advance his career. Washington was an ongoing self-constructed project. Self-improvement was important to him. He never entirely vanquished his insecurity over his lack of a college education, but he used it to fuel his reading and acquisition of knowledge.

Washington was ill at ease in the company of strangers, but he found it much easier to relax in the company of women, especially his younger female relatives. As a boy, he practiced his handwriting until it was so legible that historians today remark on how easy it is to read. He had severe life-long dental problems, exacerbated by a habit of cracking nuts with his teeth. And though he was famously reserved and made an effort not to show his emotions in public, he felt things deeply, and was prone to tears during tense or highly charged moments. In other words, he was a flawed and vulnerable human being who established an extraordinary legacy through great personal sacrifice. America would not be the nation it is today without him, but he was, first and foremost, a man: one who strived to be great, but above all, one who strived.